Should A Christian Prosper?

APOSTLE DR. DEXTER JAMES

Dexter James Impartation Ministry
Email: thewealthambassador@hotmail.com
Telephone: 1-868-289-4325

All scripture quotations are taken from the King James Version of the Bible unless otherwise stated.

ISBN: 978-1-7328555-0-2

Printed in Trinidad and Tobago

This book was written for my fellow Christian brothers, sisters and ministers in the Lord who are down and out, and perhaps a bit confused about God's promises for their lives. It also further encourages those who are already experiencing His promises.

1Chronicles 4:9-10- "*And Jabez was more honorable than his brethren: and his mother called his name Jabez, saying, because I bare him sorrow.*

And Jabez called on the God of Israel, saying, oh that thou wouldest bless me indeed, and enlarge my coast, and that thine hand might be with me, and that thou wouldest keep me from evil, that it may not grieve me! And God granted him that which he requested."

TABLE OF CONTENTS

CHAPTER ONE

What Does It Mean To Prosper?

In order to find out what it means to prosper, let us look at the origin of the word **prosper**. The word "prosper" in the Hebrew language is "tsaw-lakh" or "tsaw-lay-akh". It means to push forward, breakdown, come mighty, go over, be good, be profitable, prosperous, prosperity, prosperously.

When the children of Israel crossed the red sea they prospered; **they crossed over**. When they crossed the river of Jordan they prospered; **they crossed over**. They also prospered when they defeated their enemies whilst sickness came upon the Egyptians, but not on them and also when God answered their prayers.

Let us look at Abraham:- Anything he put his hands to do increased and he prospered until he died.

Joseph is another example of prosperity. Wherever he was, prosperity surrounded him and those around him.

Child of God, to prosper does not necessarily mean you have to be in a nice place, where everyone favors you. Joseph was not in the best of places when he prospered. You too can prosper regardless of your position in life, regardless of the circumstances against you or the situation in which you are placed. All you need to do is bring your increase (profits) into God's store-house (the church) and prove Him on His Word. **(Malachi 3:10-11)**

To prosper in life means to: - make progress, to advance, to move forward, to increase, to excel.

I want you to know something child of God, you were wired by Daddy to advance, you were wired by Daddy to make progress, you were wired by Daddy to move forward, you were wired by Daddy to increase, you were wired by Daddy to excel, you are anointed by God to do this, you are called by God to have this. Child of God to prosper is ordinary in the Kingdom of God.

CHAPTER TWO

Is It God's Will For A Christian To Prosper?

Yes, it is God's will for a Christian to prosper. Throughout the bible, God commanded His people to prosper in all that they put their hands to. The bible stated that Abraham was very rich, Genesis **13:2:- "*And Abram was very rich in cattle, in silver, and gold.*"** Now we are talking about a man that God called His friend who was very rich, and God was the one responsible for making His friend Abraham rich **(prosperous).** Now I found it a little strange for Jesus to call us His friends yet we act as if He is allergic to prosperity because a vast majority of the body of Christ still do not believe that it is God's will for them to prosper beyond what they can ask or think. **Let me just tell you what I think will happen in these last days when God begins to prosper His people; it will be prosperity unlimited, there will be no end to it, we will be caught up being a blessing to this world, we are not leaving here broke.**

Let us look at someone else who the bible declares him to be an upright man and one that fears God and yet he was wealthy and God had no problem with him being wealthy. **Job 1:1-3:- "*There was a man in the land of Uz, whose name was Job; and that man was perfect and upright, and one that feared God and eschewed evil. And there were born unto him seven sons and three daughters. His substance also was seven thousand sheep, and three thousand***

camels, and five hundred yoke of oxen, and five hundred she asses, and a very great household; so that this man was the greatest of all the men of the east."

Now it was God who prospered this upright man and even the devil knew that it was God who blessed and prospered Job. **Job 1:10:-** ***"Hast not thou (GOD) made a hedge about him, and about all that he hath on every side? Thou hast blessed the work of his hands, and his substance increased in the land."***

What happened to Job was not because he was special, but because he was a righteous man, which tells me that being prosperous could and should happen to every born again, spirit filled, God fearing believer based on the Psalmist declaration in **Psalm 1:1-3:-** ***"Blessed is the man that walketh not in the counsel of the ungodly, nor standeth in the way of sinners, nor sitteth in the seat of the scornful. But his delight is in the law of the Lord; and in his law doth he meditate day and night. And he shall be like a tree planted by the rivers of water, that bringeth forth his fruit in his season; his leaf also shall not wither; and whatsoever he doeth shall prosper."***

Righteousness and prosperity are associated, they live in the same house, they are relatives and they come from the same Father who is our heavenly Father. Therefore, the same God that declares you righteous is the same God that declares you prosperous.

Now let us look at a powerful statement used by Daddy **(Jehovah Jireh) in Deuteronomy 8:18:-** ***"But thou shalt remember the Lord thy God: for it is he that giveth thee power to get wealth."***

Now, we see it is God that is prospering His people and since we are God's people and we need plenty of money now on earth to do things for the Lord, to take care of our families and to meet our personal needs, every Christian needs to prosper. The bible stated that we are Abraham's seed by faith. As children of God, we must understand that all truth is parallel. Let us look into the natural realm where a good father, who is prosperous in business, will always encourage his children to follow in his footsteps, and ensure their prosperity. Now, look at our heavenly Daddy with me for a moment as I ask the question: Is God's word prosperous? The answer is yes. God's will is for His children to prosper.

The bible in 3 John verse 2 states: - "***Beloved, I wish above all things that thou mayest prosper and be in good health, even as thy soul prospereth."***

In 2 Chronicles 26:5, it says that "God made him (Uzziah) to prosper."

Genesis 39:3 says of Joseph, "The Lord made all that he did to prosper in his hand." Child of God, Daddy's will is that you prosper in all that you put your hands to; business, exam, church, ministry, health, marriage, family life, finances and the list goes on and on.

A PROPHECTIC WORD

I CAN HEAR JESUS SAY, "TAKE THE WILL THAT I HAVE LEFT FOR YOU, FOR I HAVE ALREADY DIED, RISEN AND I'M ABOUT TO RETURN. PROSPER TODAY, FOR YOUR PROSPERITY IS ALREADY SEALED. THE WILL IS FOR YOU, WHO ARE IN THE FAMILY OF JESUS CHRIST. YES, TAKE IT AND GLORIFY ME WITH IT, FOR YOU ARE PROSPEROUS. YOU WANT A GOOD HOME, A NICE JOB, A POWERFUL MINISTRY. DO NOT BE AFRAID OF BIG AND NICE THINGS, THAT IS MY NATURE, I AM A GOD OF EXCELLENCE," SAYS GOD.

Child of God, you must understand that we bring pleasure to Daddy **(God**) when we prosper. This is what the psalmist David says about God's response to His people's prosperity.

Psalm 35:27:- "Let them shout for joy, and be glad, that favor my righteous cause: yea, let them say continually, let the Lord be magnified, which hath pleasure in the prosperity of his servant."

God is pleasured when we prosper, God dislikes decrease, He does not tolerate slothfulness or unprofitable people. In Matthew 25:14-

30, Jesus rebukes the unprofitable servant and cast him into outer darkness where there is weeping and gnashing of teeth, however He commended the prosperous (profitable) ones and prospered them even more. So we see, it is the will of God to prosper His people.

CHAPTER THREE

People who served God and prospered in the bible

Abraham: The bible says this about Abraham in James 2:23:- ***"And the scripture was fulfilled which saith, Abraham believed God, and it was imputed unto him for righteousness: and he was called the friend of God."***

In Genesis 13:2:- this is what the bible says about God's friend Abraham. ***"And Abram was very rich in cattle, in sliver and in gold."*** Jesus calls us friends, we too can become rich. The bible also says we are Abraham's seed if we are in Christ. Saints, if having money or plenty of material things is wrong, then Abraham would have never been God's friend. He would have been God's enemy.

Isaac: In Matthew 22:32:- it states this and God is speaking. ***"I am the God of Abraham, the God of Isaac."*** And when we look at Genesis 26:12-14 this is what it records about Isaac, who said God was his God. ***"Then Isaac sowed in that land, and received in the same year a hundredfold: and the Lord blessed him. And the man waxed great, and went forward, and grew until he became very great: For he had possession of flocks, and possession of herds, and great store of servants: and the Philistines envied him."***

The bible said ***and God blessed him***, which meant God empowered him to have success, to prevail, to advance, and to move forward.

Jacob: Laban, a false god worshipper, is telling Jacob this in Genesis 30:27:- ***"And Laban said unto him (Jacob), I pray you, if I have found favor in your eyes, tarry: for I have learned by experience that the Lord has blessed me for your sake***" Verse 30 NASB this is what Jacob said to Laban; ***" for you had little before I came and it has increased to a multitude. And Lord has blessed you wherever I turned."***

God said that He is the God of Jacob also in Matthew 22:32. And we see that he too prospered in whatever he did.

Joseph: In Genesis 39:2-5, this is the record of Joseph's life. ***"And the Lord was with Joseph, and he was a prosperous man, and he was in the house of his master the Egyptian. And his master saw that the Lord was with him, and that the Lord made all that He did to prosper in his hand. And Joseph found grace in his sight, and he served him: and he made him overseer over his house, and all that he had he put into his hand. And it came to pass from the time that he made him overseer in his house, and over all that he had, that the Lord blessed the Egyptian's house for Joseph's sake ; and the blessing of the Lord was upon all that he had in the house, and in the field."*** The bible stated it clearly, that the Lord was with Joseph and he was a prosperous man. The bible said that Potiphar was able to recognize that God is with the man, and he made whatever he was involved in prospered. Saints anyone who the Lord is with should be having undeniable and unstoppable success and prosperity in their lives.

Hezekiah: This is what the bible said about Hezekiah in 2 kings 18:7, Berean study bible. ***"And the Lord was with Hezekiah, and he prospered wherever he went*"** That means if God is with me, I should prosper where ever I go. It also mean wherever I go, prosperity goes with me. Therefore, it does not matter how a place is before I enter, it has to prosper when I show up.

Uzziah: This is what is recorded in 2 Chronicles 26:5:- ***"And he sought God in the days of Zechariah, who had understanding in the visions of God: and so as long as he sought the Lord, God made him to prosper."*** As long as Uzziah sought God, God made him to prosper. Saints, seeking God will connect you to prosperity.

David: The bible said in Acts 13:22, NIV ***"After removing Saul, he made David their king. God testified concerning him: I have found David son of Jesse, a man after my own heart; he will do everything I want him to do."*** This is what 1 Chronicles 29:28 says about this man after God's own heart, ***"He (DAVID) died at a good age, having enjoyed long life, wealth and honor."***

Saints when you have the things of God first in your heart, wealth, honor and long life will locate you.

Solomon: In 2 Chronicles 1:12:- ***"Wisdom and knowledge is granted unto thee; and I will give thee riches, and wealth, and honour, such as none of the kings have had that have been before thee, neither shall there be any after thee have the like."***

God gave Solomon riches, and God wants to give you riches also. Position yourself and believe it and walk into it, for this is your time, day and hour.

Job: Job 1:1-2:- ***"There was a man in the Land of Uz, whose name was Job; and that man was perfect and upright, and one that feared God, and eschewed evil. And there were born unto him seven sons and three daughters. His substance also was seven thousand sheep, and three thousand camels, and five hundred yoke of oxen, and five hundred she asses, and a very great household; so that this man was the greatest of all the men of the east."*** This man served God and feared God and he was the richest man in his area. Saints, may our eyes open up to what God has available for those who really love Him. We know the account of job's life, he lost almost everything he had, but in job chapter forty two and verse ten, the Lord gave him twice as much as he had before. If those who serve God are supposed to be poor, why should God give Him more than he had before?

The early church: In Acts 4:34 said this. ***"Neither was there any among them that lacked: for as many as were possessors of lands of houses sold them, and brought the prices of the things that were sold."***

If Christians are supposed to be poor, why did the early church have no lack? How then did people have houses and land and were able to sell and sow the money into the kingdom of God? that the apostles were able to help the less fortunate in the congregation and kill the spirit of lack and poverty from among them.

Command for Rich Christians. This is what the bible says in 1 Timothy 6:17-18, ***"Charge them that are rich in this world, that they be not highminded, nor trust in uncertain riches, but in the living God, who giveth us richly all things to enjoy, that they do good, that they be rich in good works, ready to distribute, willing to communicate."***

If Christians should be poor and were expected to be poor, why would Paul tell Timothy to talk to those who are rich in the church about their responsibilities, letting them understand how to handle money and to understand their purpose for being rich.

CHAPTER FOUR

Why Am I Not Prospering?

Let me share with you eight reasons you may not be prospering:

1. Not Knowing The Will Of God Concerning Prosperity

If you do not know the will of God concerning prosperity, you will not prosper God's way. In **HOSEA 4:6,** God said something through His prophet that really hurts, here is the statement, **"My people are destroyed for lack of knowledge."** Do you know why millions of born again Christians are broke or poor? It is because they do not know the will of God concerning prosperity. Some even go so far to reject the knowledge of prosperity, that they hate what they label as prosperity preachers, not understanding that they themselves got saved as a result of the soul prosperity message. There are different aspects of prosperity and God's will is for us to know about all and become partakers of all and enjoy all. Therefore, not knowing the will of God concerning prosperity can be one of those reasons why you are not prospering.

2. Disobedience

Disobedience can be one of those reasons why you are not prospering. In **Deuteronomy 28:15 –68** the Bible says, **" But it shall come to pass, if thou will not hearken unto the voice of the Lord thy God, to observe to do all his commandments and his**

statutes which I commanded thee this day; that all these curses shall come upon thee, and overtake thee." When there is disobedience, which is sin, God cannot prosper the guilty one.

3. Hidden or Un-confessed Sins

Hidden or un-confessed sins can be one of those reasons why you are not prospering. The bible says in **Proverbs 28:13-: "He that covereth his sins shall not prosper, but whosever confesseth and forsaketh them shall have mercy."**

Now there are people who sin or live in sin who will not repent and expect God to prosper them. They are shacked up, drinking alcohol like if it is going out of style, using obscene language, stealing, lying, fornicating and committing adultery. God will never bless sin, you need to repent of your sin or sins and the God who is faithful and just, He will forgive you of all your sins and all unrighteousness. Why not clean up now? If there is something not right between you and Daddy, make it right now, ask Him to clean you up and ask Him to forgive you. The wise repent and the foolish die in their sins.

4. Failing To Choose To Prosper

Failing to choose to prosper can be one of those reasons why you are not prospering. **Deuteronomy 30:19:- "I call heaven and earth to record this day against you, that I have set before you life and**

death, blessing and cursing: therefore choose life that both thou and thy seed may live."

You have to choose to prosper and you do that by doing the things that God has instructed you to do in His word. If not, you will not prosper God's way.

5. Being a Non-Tither

Refusing to bring the tithe into the storehouse (the church) can be one of the reasons why you are not prospering. **Malachi 3:8-9:- "Will a man rob God? Yet ye have robbed me. But ye say, wherein have we robbed thee? In tithes and offering, ye are cursed with a curse: for you have robbed me."**

6. Holding Back

Withholding more than is meet **(right)** can be one of the reasons why you are not prospering. **Proverbs 11:24:- "There is that scattereth, and yet increaseth; and there is that withholdeth more than is meet, but it tendeth to poverty."**

7. Refusing To Follow Instructions

Refusing an instruction or instructions from God or a man of God, can be one of the reasons why you are not prospering. **Proverbs 13:18:-**

"Poverty and shame shall be to him that refuseth instruction."

8. Speaking Wrong

Speaking lack, want and need over and into your life can be one of reasons why you are not prospering. **Proverbs 6:2:- "Thou art snared (trap) with the words of thy mouth, thou art taken with the words of thy mouth."**

Testimony from the School of Prosperity

At the third session, Dr James was teaching on the subject ***the offering that breaks the curse****. While listening to him, the Holy Spirit told me to put $100.00 in his hand. I was very hesitant because I know the financial situation that I am in and to part with that money would be a strain for me. However, in my heart I knew I did not want to be disobedient. My eyes filled with tears, I took the money out. I got up from my seat and placed it in Dr James's hand and went back to my seat. He said the Lord told him something broke over my life and I knew it was true. The next day I went to someone who I owed some money. The person told me they will not bother with the money owed to them anymore. I didn't have to pay. I thank God one of my debts was cancelled because of obedience.*

CHAPTER FIVE

What Should I Do To Prosper?

Doing these seven things will cause you to prosper:

1. **Loving God**

The Bible declares in **Psalms 122:6:- "They shall prosper that love thee."** Though David was talking about Jerusalem, you've got to understand the time and season he used this term. The only nation God was concerned with was Jerusalem. Therefore to love God is to love Jerusalem **(the church)**.

I would like to state that before you start thinking about prospering, ensure that your love for God is real and that there is a deep love for the work of God in your local church, in your nation and around the world. When we read the bible, all the holy people who prospered loved God first. Abraham was a good example because he loved, feared and put God first in his life. God blessed, multiplied and increased (prospered) him. **Genesis 22:1-19.**

Matthew 6:33 says:- " But seek ye first the kingdom of God, and all his righteousness; and all these things (material things) shall be added unto you."

Love always causes one to give. God gave His only begotten son out of love **John 3:16 :- " For God so loved the world that he gave his only begotten son."**

2. **Obedience**

When you are obedient to God's word, both **"logos"** **(the written word)** and **"rhema" (the spoken word)**, you will prosper. **In Deuteronomy 28:1 God says, "And it shall come to pass, if thou shall hearken diligently unto the voice of the lord thy God, to observe and to do all his commandments which I command thee this day, that the lord thy God will set on high above all the nations of the earth.**"

As a child of God, if you follow His way, He will command the blessings upon you and you will prosper. You must live the God-fearing life to command the blessings. I want you to remember this statement before we go one step forward:

" Love gives and obedience does."

3. Tithing

Now, some Christians take this principle for granted and think that tithing does not mean anything to God. Tithing means a lot to God because of what He wants to do for you as His partner. More so, tithing is really partnering with the God who is more than enough. When you start bringing the tithes, God starts opening His windows in heaven to pour out a blessing on you. I do not know about you but I want to live under God's open windows as He pours out blessings. **Malachi 3:10:- " Bring ye all the tithes into the**

storehouse, that there may be meat in mine house, and prove me now herewith, saith the Lord of hosts, if I will not open you the windows of heaven, and pour you out a blessing, that there shall not be room enough to receive it."

"I WANT TO PROSPHESY TO YOU, THAT THIS IS THE NOT ENOUGH ROOM GENERATION. THERE ARE GOING TO BE KINGDOM AMBASSADORS WHO WILL MOVE HEAVEN WITH THEIR GIVING AND GOD WILL SEE THEIR HEARTS ARE FOR HIM AND HE IS GOING TO MAKE WHAT ABRAHAM, WHAT ISSAC AND JOB HAD LOOK LIKE POCKET CHANGE BECAUSE HE IS ABOUT TO DO IT. THE WEALTH TRANSFERANCE IS NOT COMING IT IS HERE NOW, SAITH THE LORD, MONEY ON SPIRITUAL CHARIOTS, MONEY ON EAGLE WINGS IT IS COMING LIKE THE WIND. SUPERNATURAL INCREASE SAITH THE LORD GOD OF ABUNDANCE, OPEN YOUR EYES MY PEOPLE THIS IS A BIG DAY FOR THE BODY OF CHRIST WITH BIG RESPONSIBILITIES SAITH THE LORD OF HOST."

Now, I want you to understand the terms used by the Holy Ghost in the prophecy above ***on eagle wings***, and ***chariots*** is speaking here about the speed the money will be coming.

4. Giving

Now, as a child of God you do not work for a living, you live by giving. This is one of the word that the Lord has spoken to me that has really changed my life. Here is the word**: the way you give, will determine how you live and if anybody that knew me before and see me now will tell you how I give**. Now I am not saying not to work because the bible says if a man does not work he should not eat but the bible also says work that you may have something to give not live.

Here are some scriptures to look up **(2Thess 3:10, Eph 4:28, 2Cor 9:6, Prov 11:24, Prov19: 17).**

Testimony

Now here is a testimony from my associate who was my assistant at the time when this miracle took place. After I preach about God responding to us when we pray and the blessing of God, he sow a hundred dollars into my life. The next day when he went to work he received a large increase in his salary. Now regardless of how much he worked, that was not going to happen like that, his money was sown into the anointed which went to work on his behalf that same night and brought him a harvest the next day. Let me share a next testimony with you: I was at church in Mafeking preaching and I was instructed to lift an offering which I did. There was a woman that was believing God for a house for long time after sowing her seed (money), the house was released a short while after. Giving works, it will cause you to prosper.

5. Laboring

A lazy man or woman will not prosper God's way but a man or woman who loves laboring and labors will prosper. **Proverbs 13:11:- "But he that gathereth by labor shall increase (prosper)."**

6. Talking Prosperous

Now when I use the term talking prosperous, I am talking about saying what the bible says about you and wealth or prosperity. This is what Solomon says about our words in **Proverbs 12:14:- "A man shall be satisfied with good by the fruit of his mouth.**

Proverbs 18:21:- "Death and life are in the power of the tongue: and they that love it shall eat the fruit thereof."

You might not have a dollar bill presently but talk prosperous now, be glad for other people who are prospering now, because most of those people who are prosperous now and continuing to prosper, had their share of lack and poverty. However, they made up their minds that they will believe God's word, talk big and give big out of what little they had. Therefore, on your journey to prosperity, talk big and give big and you are going to have big results.

7. Believe in Receiving

Now you can give all you know to give and still stay poor if you do not believe God to do His part; which is giving back to you. This is one hundred percent(100%) scriptural. Here are some scriptural references **Luke 6:38, 2Cor 2:9, Prov 19:17, Mal 3: 10. That's how you prosper.**

Powerful Testimonies

1. My husband sowed $1000.00 seed at Pastor Abadeen's church where he received a covenant wealth connector pin. In three days he received $15,000.00 in back pay.

2. I received a prophecy last Monday by Apostle Dexter James about a promotion on my job. I really thought that by April or mid- year it would actually come to pass. Lovely people I would like to testify to God's goodness, it's only seven days of my prophecy and I received my promotion today. Glory to God!

CHAPTER SIX

When Would I Begin To Prosper?

I must let you know for sure, God is a 'now' God, but you must not allow the process of receiving His promises make you feel like nothing is happening. Whenever God begins to answer your prayers, your prosperity starts. As you act upon the principle of God's word and from the moment you make your move according to His promise, you are in what I call the 'now process'. You may not be exactly sure what that means, so let's look into the natural for a minute:

One day while browsing through a magazine, you saw something that you liked and decided to call the store and purchase the item. The sales person assured you that the item would be delivered to you. Now, there is an interval from the time you were promised the item and the time it reaches your home. There is paper work to be done, the item has to be located and inspected, transportation arranged, and the item has to be carefully put on the vehicle taking it to your home. During all these procedures, which take time, you patiently await the delivery with great anticipation. However, if the delivering transport meets heavy traffic, or it breaks down or some other hindrance or difficulty takes place, the delivery takes longer than you expected. You then start to get impatient, anxious and worried, doubting the company's word. These are some of the things and "hiccups" the 'now process' entails As it is in the natural so it is in the spiritual.

Daniel is a perfect example of the ‘now process’. He prayed for twenty one (21) days before the answer came through to him. God heard and answered Daniel’s prayer from day one (1)) **(Daniel 10:12-14)** but interference (“hiccups”) from principalities blocked the answer. Even though Daniel wasn’t aware of this, he had patience, kept faith and waited on God. However, there are times that the proceedings are short, there are no “hiccups” and you receive the item at the promised time, and sometimes before you expect. As it is in the natural so it is in the spiritual. God does not want us to get weary and give up, wait for Him He will show up right on time.

Jesus cursed a fig tree in **Mark 11:20-24,** yet there was no visible change in the fig tree until the next day. When a disciple drew it to Jesus’ attention, he replied “Have faith in God”. In essence, Jesus was saying that the fig tree had died since the previous day. The one day interval was a completion of the ‘now process’. To walk in the fullness of God’s abundance, there is no short cut. The “now process” I am talking about is the moment you act upon God’s word. Let us look at two (2) ‘now’ statements in the bible:

God says in **Malachi 3:10:- “Bring ye all the tithes into the storehouse, that there may be meat in my house and prove me now, here with says the Lord of the host, if I will not open the windows of heaven and pour you out a blessing that there shall**

not be room enough to receive it." Act upon God's word and begin to prosper now.

These are requirements which precede the prosperity of the 'now process". Verses 8 and 9 tells what they are. There are blessings that also follows the 'now process' verses 11 and 12.

Let us look in **Psalm 118:25.** The Psalmist David is saying, **"Save now, I beseech thee, send now prosperity."** God is saying go forth, for I will be with thy mouth and teach thee what thou shall say.

Prosper now with the singing ministry, go forth and make that **CD** now. You, with that prophetic ministry go forth and speak now. You, with that broken home and is discouraged, be strong for God is able to restore all things. You can prosper in your family relationship, your children can be saved, and your business can be lifted off the ground now. I reiterate that God is a 'now' God and He is saying to His people as He said to Moses, **"now, go and prosper for I will be with you."**

Testimony

I give God thanks this morning for the powerful ministry of Apostle Dexter James .Last week I sowed a prophet's reward seed of $1041.00 believing the Lord for my ministry trip to Hawaii. The Apostle prayed and declared a miracle. Yesterday, the Lord allowed *my students to gracefully sow into my life also a distant family member which amounted to 10,000.00 for my trip. The Lord is indeed using Apostle to equip and teach the Body of Christ the importance of sowing with expectation. Thank you Apostle for your prayer of agreement.*

CHAPTER SEVEN

What Should I Do When I Begin To Prosper?

I advocate doing just as the children of God did in the book of Acts. Let's observe what they did. After Peter received the baptism of the Holy Spirit, he preached a sermon (he gave of himself); approximately three thousand (3000) were saved because he prospered (Spiritually and numerically) in the upper room.

You may say, Apostle James, you are taking this prosperity thing too far! No I am not carrying it too far. Prosperity is not just about mean or material wealth. **Luke 12:15; Colossians 3:2** indicate that it means to increase to be profitable. To increase in favor with God and man, increase to the benefit of the church and the world.

Peter was in the upper room with the other disciples when they prayed for a disciple to replace Judas: God answered their prayer- **Acts 1** (numerical prosperity). The lame man was healed (physical prosperity) when Peter said, **"In the name of Jesus Christ of Nazareth, rise up and walk."** Peter said something that moved me. Before he prayed for the man, he said. **"Silver and gold have I none, but such as I have I give unto thee."** The word **give** is the **key word** in this verse. When you begin to prosper in your ministry, your motive must not be to receive from man but from God to give to man. See references: **Luke 6:38; Acts 20:35.**

The next thing that took place, the people sold their possessions and goods and parted them to all men as every man had need **(Acts 2:45).** They gave not just a little, but to meet the need of the person. **Acts 4:34-35** says that they sold houses and land and brought the prices and laid it at the apostles' feet, and the apostle distributed to everyone according to his need. I am making a bold statement, for I believe in rightly dividing the word of truth. All churches should assist the needy in their congregation, according to the book of Acts.

I have heard a lot of messages about laying the prices (money) at the apostles' feet but not the distribution part. I am tired of the money lovers and non-people givers. Let me tell you what the Lord said to me once: Son, you are to give to the people and not take from the people. Then, we as ministers are not qualified to preach giving until we ourselves begin to practice it.

Acts 4:36-37:- "And Joses who was called Barnabas. Having land sold it and brought the money and laid it at the apostles' feet." You must begin the giving life so that you can (continue) to prosper. In the entire book of Acts, the giving principle is manifested: they gave their lives for the gospel, they gave their time to prayer and fasting, they gave their monies to help their brothers and sisters and to support the kingdom of God. Always remember to help the needy in church; encourage them to seek employment (once they are physically fit) and give rightfully so they can prosper. Reference text- 2 Corinthians 9:7; Proverbs 11:24-25.

CHAPTER EIGHT

Why Should A Christian Prosper?

Here are some keys reasons why we are as Christians should prosper:

1. Because it is God's promise to us. In **Deuteronomy 28:1-14**, God says, "All these blessings I will command upon thee." Jesus says in **Matthews 6:33:- *"Seek ye first the kingdom of God, and his righteousness; and all these things shall be added unto you."***

What does Jesus say will happen when we give? In **Luke 6:38:- *" it shall be given unto you: good measure, pressed down, shaken together and running over shall men give into your bosom. For with the same measure that you mete withal it shall be measure to you again."*** **Deuteronomy 8:18 and 29:9** declare respectively ***"But thou shall remember the Lord thy God: for it is He that gives thee power to get wealth, that he may establish his covenant which he sware unto thy fathers, as it is this day; keep therefore the words of this covenant and do them, that ye may prosper in all that you do."*** God says in **Malachi,** when we bring our tithes into His storehouse, He will open the windows of heaven and pour us out a blessing, that there shall not be room enough to receive it. God's will for us is to live in the place of ***not enough room to receive it*** and that's where I am heading in Jesus name without fail.

2. Because God finds pleasure in the prosperity of His servants- **Psalms 35:27**

3. Because the world has to see that our God can take care of us , Isaiah 60:1 speaks of the glory of the Lord being risen upon thee, the Hebrew word for glory here is kaw-bode which means be rich, heavy (in a good sense), be honorable. The psalmist says in Psalms 37:25:- "I have been young and now am old; yet have I not seen the righteous forsaken, nor his seed begging bread."

4. We need to prosper in order to fulfil this great commission: Go ye into all the world and preach the gospel to every creature. The only way we can do this effectively is when God's people begin to prosper spiritually, financially, numerically, and give towards the work of God, so that we can change families, cities, nations and the world for Jesus. Don't be afraid of what you see now, but know for sure that God's will shall come to pass in your life if you remain faithful to Him, and act on the promises in His word.

Remember, when you think of the word prosper, know that God loves His word and we must love what He loves because He created prosperity. So confess this out loudly ***I shall make my God happy so I will prosper, I am wired on the inside to prosper, I am anointed to prosper, I am sentenced for life to prosper as a child of God, I declare there is a life sentence on my life and that life sentence is life time in prosperity.***

GO AND PROSPER IN EVERY AREA OF YOUR LIFE: Spiritually, financially, mentally, physically, economically, numerically and socially.

CHAPTER NINE

My Personal Testimony

I was a security officer working for three dollar ***($3.00)*** *an hour, I accepted Jesus Christ as my Lord and saviour* ***(my entrance to prosperity, my soul began to prosper).*** *I also used to suffer with terrible migraine headaches. I was healed and I never suffered with that again (****my health began to prosper****). After about a month and a half I received another job as a checker so I was no longer employed with the security company. I was working for about six dollars and twenty-five cents* ***($6.25)*** *an hour which was a small amount still. One day the Lord spoke to me about tithing and he said to me son if you do not pay your tithes I will not be able to bless you the way I want to bless you and I started paying my tithes but there was still something wrong I was still poor, broke, in debt.*

You see no one taught me what to expect God to do for me when I paid my tithes. After several years I got married on ***mercy*** *because I was broke. I paid for everything with my credit card, but one day while I was dressing to the go to the house of God* ***(what a good place to go)*** *the Lord spoke to me and said son there is an anointing in the natural to prosper. Now before I go any further I want you to know this was new to me I never heard that before. He said look at Daniel, look at Abraham, look at Joseph and at that very moment I* *believe the anointing of prosperity came upon me. I start paying more than my tithes, hundreds of dollars more. As I write this revised edition of should A Christian Prosper, I am tremendously blessed that I am a manager in the company where I can pay my bills, I have several investments, I have my wife and I sow thousands of dollars in the kingdom of God. Now when I say thousands, I literally mean thousands and sometimes at one time. I am also an author of several books that sell and I have great favor with people in power. I can tell anybody God's word is true and it works. I want to tell you a little secret as my kingdom friends we are going to change people lives, I am on my way to become a kingdom ambassador trillionaire in Jesus name Amen.*

I want to leave you with this little advice, pay your tithes, give your offering (sow large seed) live right and expect to receive from the God who cannot lie and will not lie.

Some powerful testimonies from people who have sowed into the ministry.

1. *Hello Apostle James,*

Allow me to share what a blessing you and your ministry have been to me. It is truly tested good grounds to sow into. Back in November after consistent sowing, you said to me, you saw where God was heaping together my seeds and by Christmas 2014 I was going to receive a breakthrough. Indeed my family turned over more than an acre of land to me. While on my personal fast I was led to sow a seed *again of $320.00usd. I received an increase in salary, where I wasn't even due for an evaluation till March. Plus I found over $700.00usd near my car unexpectedly. I also heard you on the radio one night and sowed a connector seed of $1000.00tt in January. I just received a tax refund of over $400.00usd. Thank you Apostle for your continuous prayer and declarations. Blessings to you always.*

2. A man of God sowed a $1000.00 usd in my life about three weeks ago. He testifies of a $10,000.00 usd return. And seeing that it is working he is ready to sow again which is wise.

3. Last night in St Kitts, the apostle shared a testimony. He said when I was in St. Kitts at the Apostolic Faith Missions for a financial conference, I asked the people to sow a $500.00 ec. He said they were about to start building their church and had just open a bank account. They were gathering up the money. He said he sowed the $500.00 ec and two week later he received $10,000.00 ec. To date they have received $80,000.00 for their building project and are continuing the building. Do not tell me it does not work.

4. A business man testified after sowing seeds for his businesses. He said that an American company owed him over a million dollars for more than two years. They never responded to his requests for payment but after taking the challenge to sow the seed, he received a text message that they would come to sort payments out. This is what the anointing does.

5. Apostle Dexter James visited our church in Louisiana for Trouble in the City. He challenged us to sow $1000.00usd seed. A young man from another church came and sowed this seed. He believed God for favour to purchase a rental property. He has now bought and flipped his first property and presently just purchased another house. Somebody ought to shout right here.

6. Never have second thoughts towards sowing especially if it is your last set of cash. Apostle Dexter James told us not to worry, money would flow before Wednesday. Mines started flowing from Monday straight until today; I was like wow. I was never worried when I gave my last set of cash. I knew God would have provided, but he surprised me big time. Always obey Guys.

7. A woman testified that she sowed sacrificially which was half of her grocery money at a meeting. The next night someone gave her twice the amount she sowed .Someone else also gave her groceries and is assisting her with her children's school books.

8. A pastor wanted a new A/C unit in her office because the present one was not working. She sowed the Wednesday night and by Friday someone installed a new A/C unit in her office. I do not know about you but I know about me. I am fully persuaded that sowing and reaping works.

9. Good night Apostle on February 28th I attended your debt free conference in Cascadia Hotel where I sowed a seed towards my debt *of $41,000.00. You said in 10 months we would get results. I continued sowing into your ministry and I received two unexpected cheques. Today I went to the bank and cleared all monies. I am now debt free. Thank you for teaching us. God's richest blessings upon you.*

10. Apostle Dexter I had the pleasure of meeting you last year in Laplace at Prophet Antonie's church. You spoke a word in my life when I sowed the seed of $700.00. I wanted you to know that just like you said that doors would open in 3 and 6 months, the doors are opened and I can't wait to see what door God opens in the 9th and 12th month. I ask that you keep me in prayer and I pray that God continues to work in my life.

11. Hi good day Apostle, I was looking for a place to open a food stall business and it was not working out. So after sowing my first fruit on Sunday I went to check out a place but more so I was looking for somewhere in front of a building to set up. There was this place I had in mind so I went there to meet the owner. He said yes when I asked him about using in front of his building. He told me he would put lights at the front of the building. The best part is when I asked him the cost of the rent; he said I can't charge you. You can start when you are ready. I said all this to say whenever I sow in your life something great always happens for me. You are good ground to sow into. Thanks.

12. Good evening Apostle James, I pray all is well with you. I am writing to share my testimony of how the Lord used you to speak into my life the last time I saw you. The word was, "Pam , because of your heart, I am giving you the ability to gain wealth." In December 2016 I received a lump sum from the US Army that allowed me to cancel the debt I had. I also purchased two vehicles to help my children. I used to be concerned about not having a retirement fund, but now I will receive compensation from the Army for the rest of my life. I just moved into my new home last week and was able to purchase a new vehicle for myself. I just wanted to thank God for His anointing on your life and for you being a servant of The Most High God.

13. Someone sowed a Solomon seed from Bishop Mc-pherson's church. He got promoted right after that without requiring qualifications in order to get that position. He would have had to return to school to get the qualification for this specific position. Seed always produces harvest.

14. Hi Apostle,You remember when you were doing the offering for one of the nights in the meeting "Let the oil flow", you started at $300usd and came all the way down .I took an envelope for $40usd.I went home and I increased it to $100usd.I wrote three things on the envelope and one of them was I needed a job. Now today I'm working at one of the most prestigious organisations in Jamaica.

15. About two months ago I bided on an order for graphic design and printing job from our parliament. My company was eventually awarded the job. But I have been back and forth with them for a while month to get the funds released to me. I got a message yesterday that I can go and collect an upfront pay of $10,000.00srd to start the job.

You dealt last night with money being delayed to be released. Mine started as from today and my money will start flowing to me. This thing works.

16. I would like to say a personal thank you to you Apostle Dexter James. I decided to obey your instructions and sow into my leader's life . Approximately three weeks later I became the owner of an acre of land and a house. Continue to pour out as your ministry impacts the lives of many believers. Now I cant stop sowing.

17. Praise God for His goodness. It is so good to touch down in a country when the first thing you are greeted with is a testimony. I prophesied to this young man about registering his business and that he will employ people to work with him. I told him that the business would be very big and not small. He reported to me that the first contract he received was for $15,000 in December 2017 and presently he received another contract for $500,000 and has two other contracts in another part of the island. In addition to this he has employed persons from his church. God is faithful. Your word too shall pass.

18. A woman of God came to me and I gave her a word of the Lord that she was going to receive twenty thousand dollars. I challenged her to sow a seed of two thousand dollars and she received this amount. To God be the Glory.

19. Good morning man of God. I thank the Lord for the anointing on your life. I was at the conference in Suriname at Bethel Upper Room at Pastor Fluke. I was the gentleman who came to sow the $500srd.I actually saw a divine acceleration after sowing this seed in my financial affairs. You had prophesied to me about a business. I tackled it and now it's the first time in my life that every Monday from the end of January I'm going to earn $27,500.00 usd per month on the basis of a contract of eighteen months. The Lord also led me to become a shareholder in a security company where I am the shareholder of 40%.Glory to Jesus our Way-Maker.

20. Dexter, Dexter, Dexter Thank you oh so much for touching my hands. I thank God for you and your gift and the many gifted alike and the obedience. Oh the obedience. How you know I needed that $100.00 usd?

You gave me $100.00 at the Mountaintop Faith Ministries in Las Vegas last year. I was broke. All I had was a dream and this $100.00 after that. You told me that the $100.00 usd was the first to the many that were to follow me wherever I went. Remember I said I had a dream. Well this dream isn't just a normal dream. What I'm doing has never been done. I needed money to manifest this dream into *reality. Not even a month after the day you touched my hands, I went from having a dream and that $100.00 usd to having $5,000.00 usd. That $100.00 usd gave birth to a successful journey. That dream I had, its manifesting into reality as I type this. Thank you.*

21. I received a word of knowledge that the Lord was dealing with someone to sow a seed of $20,000.00. I stated that when that seed is released that the person would receive $200,000.00.Please note wording that the Lord was dealing with them.

Someone informed me that while in service "the $20,000.00 seed crossed my mind as I was considering sowing the seed. Twice it crossed my mind. Even the $200,000.00 you mentioned came in a dream a few days ago, the exact amount."

22. Praise God for praise reports, I met someone named Chris and his family. He said he I wanted to see you for a long time. He said I have a testimony. Years ago I came to one of your meetings and my wife and I were experiencing financial difficulties. I came to tell you and you told me to bring all the money I have and sow it. It was $10.00tt and you prayed. Today I have three businesses, three vehicles and I purchased a home.

The real test of a financial deliverer is if he or she is willing to preach the gospel to the poor and contented with the people sowing small sacrificial seed.

23. Praise report from our 1st annual "Breaking the Back of Poverty and Healing Conference, one of our members was challenged to sow a sacrificial seed. Apostle Dexter James decreed within ten days he shall receive the increase of his seed. He called me upon yesterday. He received a new job making twice as much, with benefits and another raise within thirty days .Is your faith active?

THE END OF TESTIMONIES

Should you believe God is leading you to ***Warriors Assembly Growing Church Breakthrough Ministries***, here are our current locations in Trinidad and Tobago:

1. Princes Town (Restoration City)

Bless Avenue, New Grant, Princess Town

1 (868) 347-7180, 494-4604

2. Couva (Head Quarters)

147 Southern Main Road 1 (868) 289-4325, 388-2769

3. Aripero (House of Prophetic Destiny)

1414 Aripero Village, Rousillac

(Deo's Shopping Mall) 1 (868) 718-2697, 752-0056

4. Siparia (House of Power)

15 High Street (Upstairs KFC) 1 (868) 491-7153

Made in United States
Troutdale, OR
11/03/2026

56845108R00027